Love Is a Red and White Umbrella

Diane Simmons Dill

Love is a Red and White Umbrella

Diane Simmons Dill

ISBN: 978-0-9889811-1-9
ISBN: 978-0-9889811-0-2 (e-book)

Cover Design: Diane Simmons Dill

Edited by Patricia Simmons Taylor

Cover Photograph by Life's a Snap! Photography
Photographer: Shannon D. Bates
Models: Hayleigh Brackett and Jesse Knowles

Dedication

This book is dedicated to my family: to my loving husband, Wayne, who teaches me daily what real love is; to my amazing and beautiful daughters, Angela, Shannon, and Heather, three examples of love with whom God blessed me – I am so proud of each one of you; and to my sweet sister, Patricia, who has been a precious example of Christ's love all my life. It would be impossible to list all that each of you has done for me, so thank you all for everything you have done, everything you are still doing, and for being in my life. Pat, thank you for a lifetime of love and care, and thank you for graciously being my editor. You made the book better with your suggestions. To my other siblings, Nelle, Sonny, Elaine, Carolyn, and Jimmy, thank you for the many kind and generous acts you've done for me over the years, especially during my childhood – they are appreciated. I also want to honor the memory of my parents, John Shoemaker Simmons and Mildred Burchfield Simmons, both of whom showed love to all of us while here on Earth, and both of whom have been in Heaven for many years now. Thank you, Mother and Daddy, for your love and for all the life lessons you taught me.

I love you all, with a real love, the kind of love that comes only from our Lord and Savior, Jesus Christ. May readers be blessed, and may Christ be exalted through the words on these pages. All praise and glory forevermore to God the Father, God the Son, and God the Holy Spirit!

Table of Contents

Note: All Scriptural references are from the New International Version, unless otherwise noted.

Prologue

This book represents a lifetime of struggling to find the meaning of love. More accurately, it was a search to find the meaning of *real* love. I was raised during an era when girls were expected to grow up, fall in love, get married, have children, and ... well, those were pretty much the only expectations for little girls in the Deep South during the 1950s and 1960s. I dutifully tried to meet the expectations that society dictated. Unfortunately, I had no clue about what real love was. All I knew was that a huge hole was in my heart and soul, and all the attempts I made to find love were fruitless. I wanted to tell my story as a way to encourage anyone who might be struggling and searching for the one thing we all need the most – real love, the kind that God offers to each one of us through Jesus Christ.

My father's decision to accept the Lord as his Savior occurred when I was a teenager. Church attendance had never been a part of our family life. I remember being upset that I was now required to attend church on Sunday nights because it meant that I would miss the Ed Sullivan Show! There were no VCRs or DVRs and no TIVO during those days. It seems funny now, but missing a favorite show was a big deal to a teenager. However, hearing the Word of God preached weekly convicted my heart, and I accepted the Lord at age 16. My mother was a Christian but had not attended church for several years. When Daddy became a Christian, she rededicated her life to the Lord, and our family became regular attendees of our local church. However, since my family had not attended church during my childhood, I had very little religious instruction. Except for a few trips to church with my cousin, Beatrice (Bea), I knew almost nothing about God or His love. I thank God for Bea and her willingness to take my siblings and me to church occasionally. Once my parents and I started attending church, my Sunday school teacher was a precious lady named Ruth. She and her husband, Charles, were two of the finest examples of living a Christian life that I've ever witnessed. Ruth and Charles fairly glowed with the love of Christ. It was impossible to be around them and not see the Light of the world shining through. I can still picture Ruth's beautiful, smiling face, and the sweetness she displayed to everyone. When I get to Heaven, I can't wait to thank Bea and Ruth for planting those first few seeds of God's love in my heart.

Growing up, I thought I was part of a close-knit family, and in many ways I was. Daddy loved to laugh, and he playfully teased us just to make us laugh. When the "popsicle truck" came into our neighborhood, we knew to ask him for the money for our favorite frozen treat because he could never say no. Even though our family rarely had extra money, he would tell our mother, "Mama, give them a quarter for a popsicle." He would get sugar cane when it was in season and let us chew it to get the sweet juice out of it. I can still recall how the juice usually ended up running down my chin. Daddy also brought home sassafras root, which he brewed for tea. To this day, root beer, which is made from sassafras root or bark, is one of my favorite beverages.

Mother sewed clothes for seven kids, walking five blocks to our Aunt Mildred's house to use her sewing machine to stitch the side seams of a garment. The rest she sewed by hand with stitches so small you could barely see them. A man from our church once asked her if she had glued the pieces of a quilt that she had stitched by hand with those same tiny, precise stitches! She even sewed buttonholes by hand, so perfectly stitched that they looked better than those made by a machine. She nursed us, and half the neighborhood as well, when we were sick. When it came to making do with what was on hand, nobody could top her. She could make a meal out of what seemed like nothing, and she and Daddy both could improvise to make what they needed.

However, in hindsight I now realize that our family had some real problems, primarily due to a failure to communicate and a lack of understanding regarding emotional and spiritual needs. In some ways, ignorance was at work as well. I don't mean ignorance as in a lack of intelligence. I mean spiritual and emotional ignorance. This is the ignorance of simply not knowing the importance of spiritual instruction, and not knowing how to deal with emotions or even being aware that they needed to be addressed. One of my mother's favorite expressions when troubles threatened was, "Don't rock the boat." She was not being callous or cavalier. Avoidance and denial were the only ways she knew to cope. We did not have the benefit of God's Word as a guideline, and we were taught by example to sweep problems, hurt feelings, and most other emotions, "under the rug." In order to avoid dealing with them, we avoided discussing them. In fact, we pretended that the problems didn't exist. Like many other parents, our parents wanted peace at all cost. Unfortunately, the cost was high, and we all paid the price emotionally.

Growing up, I learned by observation that the families I knew did not openly show emotion. There were no hugs and nobody said, "I love you." My parents took care of our basic needs for food, clothing, and shelter. They taught us right from wrong, and they made sacrifices in many ways, especially our mother, who sometimes did without in order to give to her children. But the things that were left undone and unsaid sometimes outweighed the positive.

3

Life is not just about having our basic needs met. Being loved and accepted is also one of our most basic needs. If someone doesn't know how to show real love, they can't teach it to their children. It becomes a generational problem that gets passed down. The problem with not knowing the definition of real love is that we have only the world's influence and opinion to guide us. A lot of the unwise decisions and choices we make are the result of just wanting to be loved. My siblings and I were unprepared for young adulthood and beyond. When an unprepared child is thrust into the world and expected to cope and make major life decisions, the chances for problems, bad decisions, and mistakes increase exponentially. Without being taught about God's love or how to express emotions, we knew little about the importance of depending on God or how to build a healthy self-esteem. We were at the mercy of the world, and the world shows very little mercy. Ignorance is not bliss. Ignorance is an enemy to our souls because it has the potential to ruin lives.

Almost twenty years ago, I became involved with a group of people I met as the result of my close friendship with a former co-worker. She was extremely zealous about religion and her church and urged me to become a part of the congregation. At the time, I was going through a rough time emotionally and was struggling for answers, trying to understand God's plan for my life. I thought the world of my friend, and she seemed so wise spiritually. Because I trusted her, I thought her fellow church-goers were trustworthy. I eventually learned, however, that I was being used, manipulated, and lied to by all of them, including the woman I thought was my friend. Their interest in me had nothing to do with God or spiritual matters. They only wanted the money that I could put in the offering plate. They were involved with ungodly things, and I shudder to think that money I contributed in faith might have been used for ungodly purposes. I thank the Lord that He sees the intent of the heart. My faith was real, and my motives were genuine. Unlike the merciless world, God poured out His mercy upon me, for which I am deeply and eternally grateful. My sister, Pat, tried to warn me that this group of people was not what they seemed. She said the Holy Spirit was giving her a warning about these people who appeared so spiritual to me. I remember being stunned that she would say such a thing! I argued with her that she just didn't know them, that they were the most Godly people I had ever known. Thank God that Pat prayed for me to become aware of the truth. But when I did, I felt totally betrayed and was devastated. It was the equivalent of emotional blunt force trauma, and it felt as if my heart had been violently ripped out and torn into a million pieces.

At my lowest point, I couldn't eat or sleep and became so depressed that thinking clearly was impossible. I was in such emotional pain, grieving for the losses I experienced – lost friendship and lost innocence by the betrayal I experienced at the hands of those who were supposed to be friends and spiritual models. Overwhelmed, I just wanted the deep and visceral pain to stop. My health suffered, and I lost so much weight that total strangers would stop and ask me if I was all right. My Commanding Officer in the Coast Guard Reserve called me into his office and asked if I was having any problems. Co-workers were concerned about me, and Pat later told me she was worried that I would starve to death.

Finally, one night while in utter despair, I asked God to help me and to show me His truths, not some "truth" that another human being decided was true. While preachers, pastors, Sunday School teachers, and Godly friends can help increase our knowledge and help us to grow spiritually, it is up to each of us to seek the path God chooses for us. The Bible tells us to study to show ourselves approved and to work out our own salvation (Philippians 2:12, II Timothy 2:15). I told God that I wanted to know His truth, and His alone, that I was ready to depend totally on Him. I told Him I was confused and didn't know what to believe about the events I had experienced. After that fiasco, I began to wonder whether I knew anything anymore. But thankfully there was one thing that I was absolutely sure of. I was a child of God, saved by grace.

So I did the only thing I could think of. I cried out to God and told Him, "Lord, I don't know what to think, and I don't know what to do, but I know You. I know that You love me, and I know that I can trust You, so I will depend on You, Lord." Somehow I instinctively understood that if I started with what I knew, God would lead me the rest of the way. God taught me that I made two fundamental mistakes in dealing with the people who hurt me so deeply – the people that I had *allowed* into my life, for which I take full responsibility. First, I put more faith in them than I did in God, and second, I did not follow His command to "Trust in the Lord with all your heart and lean not on your own understanding. In all your ways acknowledge Him and He shall direct your paths" (Proverbs 3:5-6, NKJV). Though it pains me to admit that, it is the truth. Because I took my eyes off the Lord, I paid a high price emotionally and spiritually. However, in Genesis 50:20, God said, "You intended to harm me, but God intended it for good to accomplish what is now being done, the saving of many lives." God used that experience to strengthen my faith beyond any measure that I could have envisioned on my own. I had a hard time forgiving these people in the beginning. The hurt was so deep! One day I was reading the Bible and came across the Scripture, "But I tell you, love your enemies and pray for those who persecute you, that you may be children of your Father in heaven (Matthew 5:44-45)." I remember thinking, *but Lord, these people don't deserve forgiveness!* Instantly, the Holy Spirit whispered to me, *"Neither did you, but Jesus forgave you when you didn't deserve it, either."* Wow! Talk about a reality check! With that perspective, I was immediately able to forgive those who hurt me. I've been on quite an adventure since then. I am so grateful to God for loving me, for catching me when I was falling, and for helping me to rise again through faith in Him.

I am especially grateful for Pat, too. A wonderful sister and friend, Pat has always been in my corner. When we were children, she consistently gave me something that nobody else did, the best gift that one person can give to another – her time, her love, herself. When I went through the devastating events of twenty years ago, Pat is the one who reached out to me, let me live with her for several months, cooked meals for me, nurtured me, and loved me. When I read the Scripture in Philippians 1:3, "I thank my God upon every remembrance of you," I think of Pat. It's because of her and her faithfulness to God that I survived.

I also remember another vivid event where Pat ministered to me on a deep spiritual level. Her oldest son, Jeff, was in a motorcycle accident when he was 15 years old. He had a terrible brain injury, but after two and a half years, he seemed to finally be healing. This was in large part because of Pat's constant loving care for him. On November 16, 1983, a week before Thanksgiving, Jeff turned 18 years old. He had looked forward to turning 18 and was so excited because, as he put it, "Now I'm a man!"

In 1983, Thanksgiving fell on November 24. On November 22, Jeff went to the neurologist for a check-up, and the doctor said he was doing great. But God had other plans for Jeff and for Pat, for our whole family. Some time in the wee hours of November 23, the day before Thanksgiving, Jeff suffered a grand mal seizure and passed away. His funeral was held the day after Thanksgiving.

This catastrophic turn of events has been so very difficult for Pat and her family and for all of us. Yet in the midst of it, Pat remained faithful and clung tightly to Jesus Christ. But something happened at the time Jeff had the accident that changed my life.

I remember the shock when we got the awful news that Jeff had been seriously injured in an accident, and the doctors were saying he probably would not live through the night. Our entire extended family gathered in the hospital's waiting room. It was the only thing any of us knew to do. Nobody in our family had ever been gravely injured before. We were all just sitting there, trying to grasp the enormity of the situation. We were praying but felt helpless, grieving for what had happened.

What happened next will forever be indelibly etched into my memory. All of a sudden, Pat stood up, then knelt down, and began to pray ... out loud, pouring her heart out to the Lord. None of us had ever seen anyone do this in a public setting outside of church. Pat hadn't said anything to anybody beforehand. She just knelt down and began to fervently pray out loud, as if she were alone in her prayer closet at home. I remember every word of her prayer. She prayed for God to heal Jeff, to help him, and to watch over him. And then she told God that if there was any way He could grant her prayer for her son, that her request would be to let him live. Then she said, "but nevertheless, not my will, but Yours, Lord."

Even now that has such a profound impact on me. To know that your child is dying, and to pray for that child is one thing. But then to turn it all over to God, surrender to His will, and trust that His grace is sufficient regardless of the outcome, required total trust and faith. She would somehow get through it with the Lord's help.

It was after this happened that I started thinking about my own life and how far I had strayed from God. I began to change my life from that point on. In many ways, I feel that Pat has saved my life twice – once when Jeff was hurt, and once when I was devastated emotionally. She saved my spiritual life and my literal life.

So here we are now, and this book is finally being written. I wish I could say that I hadn't spent a major part of my adult lifetime looking for love as the world defined it for me. The truth is that I've wasted many years looking for what I thought was love. Real love – God's love – was right there, waiting for me. All I had to do was become aware of it and accept it.

I am grateful for so many things. I praise the Lord for His goodness and mercy, and for the only love that really matters – His love.

1. Seven Billion Definitions

What is the definition of love? A quick canvass of 100 people will likely yield at least 100 answers. Ask 1,000 people, and they could have at least 1,000 answers. And so it goes. It seems that love means something different to almost everyone.

To a child, it means the safety and security of having loving parents who take care of them. A teenaged girl might swoon over posters of a favorite rock star, whose image is plastered all over the walls of her room, declaring with certainty that she is "in love." To a parent, it means the closeness shared with their children.

Husbands and wives would agree that love, from their perspective, is the intimate relationship they share and the respect and affection they feel for each other. Teachers, who invest their lives to provide education and wisdom to young people, might consider the privilege of teaching to be a demonstration of love. Indeed, especially when we consider the low pay most teachers in the United States receive, teaching is a labor of love. To a soldier, knowing that a trusted brother-in-arms has his (or her) back is an example of love.

A banker might say that money – and lots of it – is love. They dream of the money they have now and the money they will have in the future. Wealthy business people sometimes share the banker's assessment of what love is. Perhaps the love of money is really at work here, yet many wealthy people also love the Lord and use their money to further the Lord's work. The Bible does not condemn money. Money is a good and necessary tool in our lives. But when we love only the money and elevate its importance above what really matters, problems arise.

If the question of what love means is posed to an attorney, the answer might be, "It all depends." In the legal world, a definition is determined by the circumstances, the people involved, the intent, and many other factors. All lawyer jokes aside, the attorney's answer is probably the closest to the truth. What does love mean? It all depends on whom you ask.

Planet Earth has over seven billion people. That means there could be at least seven billion definitions of love! As we will see, even God's Word illustrates love on more than one level.

2. What a Difference One Word Can Make!

Webster's Dictionary defines four kinds of love:

Eros is used to describe erotic love.

Philos means the kind of love we have for friends.

Storge is used to represent family love, such as the love parents have for their children, or siblings have for each other.

Agape is a very special kind of love – and the most rare. It means love that is selfless, sacrificial, and unconditional. *Agape* is the kind of love that Jesus has for us. It's why He chose to die an agonizing death on a cross to save us from sin. He thought of us rather than of Himself, He sacrificed His life for our own, and His love is unconditional. He invites us to come just as we are, without having to pay a single penny for this wondrous gift. In fact, it would be impossible for us to pay for it because Jesus has already paid the ultimate price for our sins (I Corinthians 6:20, I Peter 1:17-21).

In God's Word, all these different kinds of love are depicted. *Eros* includes physical love between a man and a woman. A good example of *eros* would be the story of Samson and Delilah in Judges 16. Another example would be in I Corinthians 7:5, which advises married couples regarding their physical relationship. The entire book, Song of Solomon, is based on *eros* between a husband and wife.

In I Samuel 18, we learn about *philos*, the kind of love between friends, like Jonathan and David. They shared a deep, brotherly love toward one another.

There are countless stories of family love in the Bible. One example is the story about a father whose young daughter died. Through his love for his daughter and his faith in Jesus, his daughter was raised from the dead (Matthew 9:18-25). Many

Scriptures, too numerous to list, talk about family love, such as how Jesus loved the Apostles and considered them family. The whole concept of salvation and Christianity is all about believers being "adopted" into the family of God (Galations 4:5, Romans 8:15-17).

In John 3:16, we see that *agape* is described: "For God so loved the world that he gave his one and only Son, that whoever believes in him shall not perish but have eternal life." God was willing to give all He had, His only Son. John 15:13 says "Greater love has no one than this: to lay down one's life for one's friends." That is exactly what Jesus did for us. Because Jesus loves us unconditionally and accepts us even when we are in a sinful state, we can accept the salvation He offers. Like any gift, love must be accepted, and when we accept the gift of God's love by asking Christ to come into our hearts, we experience *agape*.

A quote by John Harrigan says, "People need loving the most when they deserve it the least." That sums up our need for Jesus Christ, and it sums up what He did for us on Calvary's cross and what he continues to do for us through *agape*.

It is mind boggling – and humbling – to realize that God the Father, the very Creator of the entire Universe, and His precious Son, Jesus Christ, love us this much. Oh, how grateful we are for *agape* love!

3. Love Is All Around

Most people encounter love many times a day without realizing it. Love is all around us, or at least it could be. Let's take a peek into one Christian family's daily life, but to make it more interesting, here's a twist. One family, one set of circumstances, but two reactions and responses, with two very different results. We will call the two responses Scenario One and Scenario Two. First, here is some basic information about the family.

Suppose there is a woman, Janice, who is married to Todd, and they have two children, Billy and Amanda. Todd works hard to provide for his family, and they have a nice home. Janice also works outside the home, attends church with her family, and volunteers at the local soup kitchen.

Todd usually helps out where needed. In the past, he got the children ready for school when Janice was busy with something else or had to leave early for work. He does other things for the children and spends time with them. Though Janice and Todd grew up during an era where the wife and mother handled the majority of household tasks, Todd is willing to share the household and family duties. Janice and Todd both work hard to communicate, which is key to all successful relationships. By working together, they can be a good example to their children as they grow up and prepare for the future. Sometimes life and situations don't always go smoothly, as we will see later on, but when a dedicated couple depends on God and sets the example of love, it enhances their family life and prepares the children to have successful relationships in the future.

Here is Scenario One:

The day begins, and Todd kisses Janice good morning. She wakes the kids, and while they dress, she prepares their favorite breakfast, pancakes. They bow their heads to give a prayer of thanks, and while eating, they converse pleasantly about the day ahead. Even though it's Billy's turn to feed the cat, Amanda finishes breakfast before he does and offers to do it for him. Before the children leave to get on the school bus, Janice double checks their backpacks and hands them a lunch they will enjoy. As Janice dresses for work, the phone rings and a co-worker, Cathy, explains that she has a flat tire and asks if Janice could possibly "swing by" and give her a ride to work. Both Janice and Cathy know that it will be more of a two-mile detour rather than just swinging by, but Janice responds, saying, "Sure, Cathy. I can stop by and pick you up. I'll see you in about 15 minutes." She hears the relief in Cathy's voice as she says thank you. When Cathy gets in the car, she smiles, expresses her gratitude again, and hands Janice a blueberry muffin, fresh from the oven.

Janice arrives at work and savors the delicious muffin with a hot cup of coffee. She smiles, thanking God for another beautiful day.

Notice the choices made by everyone in this scenario. Admittedly, it sounds a bit like Utopia, but doesn't God command Christians to show love to one another no matter what the circumstances are? Now let's go back and replay each instance that happened in Janice's morning, but this time, let's see it from a totally different perspective. Consider how different the mindsets of Janice and her family might have been if the day had gone like this instead.

Scenario Two:

Todd gets up, dreading the staff meeting he knows is coming a little later. He barely says good morning, grunting as he passes by, not really even seeing

15

Janice. Hurt, she turns away, wondering if she has done something to make him angry. Sighing, she becomes preoccupied as she ponders what she could have done to put Todd in such a foul mood. She is vaguely aware of the morning news on TV, jarring back to reality when she hears that the time is now 7:10. She hurriedly tries to wake Billy and Amanda, but after being frantically awakened by their mother, they are not cooperative. They drag themselves into the kitchen, and Janice shoves a cold bowl of cereal at them, yelling that they need to hurry before the school bus gets there. The kids fuss and bicker, using up what's left of their breakfast time to argue over whose turn it is to feed the cat. The school bus arrives, and Janice quickly stuffs a bag of chips and an apple into each backpack, then practically slings the backpacks in the kids' direction. They stomp out of the house, with no breakfast, an inadequate lunch, and a bad attitude.

The phone rings. A quick check of caller ID indicates that it's Cathy. Not again! It seems that she calls every week with a new sob story. Her car won't start ... her husband had to work a double shift and won't be home for two more hours ... the car has a flat tire. Janice can't believe that Cathy has the audacity to ask her yet again to "swing by" and pick her up. It's a good two miles out of the way, for Pete's sake! When Cathy asks about getting a ride to work, Janice snaps at her, "No, I'm running late myself this morning, so I won't be able to pick you up. Sorry." Though she hears the hurt in Cathy's voice as she quietly says, "I understand. Thank you anyway. Sorry to bother you," Janice ignores the little prick of guilt that her conscience jabs at her. She doesn't have time to worry about someone else's problems. She has enough to worry about with trying to figure out what she did to make Todd so grumpy.

Janice arrives at work, irritated, and realizes she never ate breakfast. She sits at her desk and drinks a cup of coffee, but by now even the coffee tastes bitter. She's in such a bad mood that all she can think about is the anger she feels about how the morning has unfolded. As Cathy rushes by, disheveled and out of breath, Janice looks away, another pang of guilt washing over her for not helping Cathy get to work. Sighing, she thinks, *it's going to be another long day.*

Which one of these scenarios seems to be going in the direction of God's plan? Jeremiah 29:11 tells us, "'For I know the plans I have for you,' declares the LORD, 'plans to prosper you and not to harm you, plans to give you hope and a future.'" In the first scenario, love sets the tone for the day. Gratitude and gentleness show the love that Janice and her family have toward one another and others. The Bible tells us in Proverbs 23:7a (KJV), "For as he thinketh in his heart, so is he." It is clear that our words and actions either demonstrate love and gratitude, or they demonstrate that something is wrong with our thinking. We develop a "heart problem." A heart problem becomes a mindset problem, which becomes a spiritual problem. We can choose to show something positive or something negative, but we have to choose one. It's impossible to feel anger and gratitude at the same time.

4. Finding God's Love in Everyday Places

Like the scenarios with Janice and her family, similar episodes are played out all over the world. Both examples occur on a daily basis no matter where we live or what our individual circumstances are.

I wish I could say that my own family life unfolded the way Janice's did in the first example, but the truth is that the second scenario ruled many days of my life while raising three daughters. I look back now and cringe – so many lost opportunities to demonstrate God's love! So many chances to make life easier for my husband and children. So many regrets.

Janice and her family really do love one another, but that did not seem to be the case in the second example. The love they feel didn't change just because the day started out negatively and only got worse as the morning wore on. Their *choices* changed. The attitudes and the actions, reactions, and the things they said, or didn't say, changed. Each person had the opportunity to make a choice. We can't change other people or choose for them. Our own choices and attitudes are the only things we can change.

A wife and mother can set the mood for the day for her entire family. She holds in her hands the power to influence them, either negatively or positively. Whomever said, "If mama ain't happy, ain't nobody happy," was correct. It means that a mother's level of happiness can influence her family and their lives. It's important for her to consider the manner in which she wishes to influence how the day begins, how it progresses, and how it ends. But the mother within a family is not the only one who can influence the family's mood. The father is equally responsible to care for his family, not only with material things, but with consideration for their emotional and spiritual needs

18

as well. In fact, the Bible teaches that the man is the head of the family (I Timothy 3:4). In that role, he must take responsibility for his wife and children, to love them and help them grow spiritually. The Bible is also careful to stress that the Lord is the head of every Christian, male or female, young or old. And even Christ is subject to God (I Corinthians 11:3). As head of the woman, the man is to display *agape* toward her and their children. There are also instructions for women to display God's love. In other words, all Christians are commanded to exhibit God's love toward others (I Peter 2 and 3).

In Scenario Two, when Todd woke up and seemed grumpy, Janice could have brought a cup of coffee to him and given him a big hug. No words were necessary. Janice's actions would have spoken volumes. If Janice had been loving and kind, *even when Todd started out in the opposite direction*, Todd would have felt loved, and her presence and gestures would have reminded him that no matter what else happens, he has a family that he loves and who loves him in return. Instead of being unpleasant and avoiding Janice, he could have smiled and given her a hug in return. This would have meant so much to Janice and likely would have started her day off much more smoothly. Through their choices, either of them could have changed their mindsets, which might also have changed the mindsets of their children and Cathy.

Janice could have chosen not to jump to any conclusions about whether she had done something to make Todd angry. Even if she thought that, she could have said a quick prayer and left it up to God. For that moment, she could have remained quiet, not worried about it, and asked Todd later if anything was bothering him. Rather than worrying about the staff meeting, Todd could have spent time praying and trusting the Lord to have His hand on the situation.

Janice's preoccupation made her less than nurturing toward her children. If she had chosen to be the loving parent she tries and wants to be, the dilemma with the children might not have occurred. Todd could have sensed that Janice or the children needed encouragement and help, and he could have made a big difference in the day and in their lives.

Because of the choices made, the day's negative beginning only got worse. Each choice along the way diminished Janice's spirit of charity towards others. She was unkind and uncaring to Cathy. Instead of offering one bright spot in Cathy's morning, she chose to add one more worry to her already stressed out situation. This could have been a chance for Janice to minister to and encourage a young woman, increasing her faith and showing Christ's love to her. Instead, Janice chose to not only take away Cathy's peace and joy, but her own as well. Todd's choices also had a negative impact on his wife and children. If he had set the example of love, demonstrating patience, kindness, and dependence on God and His Word, he and his family would have benefitted tremendously.

While the wife and mother often takes the lead in family matters, especially with the children, each husband and father should share that responsibility. Obviously, each couple's situation is different. Many factors come into play. For example, many men work 10-12 hours or more every day. So do some women. Each family's circumstances are different and will dictate how much time each spouse can devote to household duties. The type of work is also a factor. If someone works hard for 10-12 hours, especially if the work is outdoors where it's hot during the summer and cold during the winter, their energy level will not be the same as someone with an 8-hour work day indoors. Many women work full time, go to school, take care of the children's needs, pay the bills, and all the other household duties that come along. Without their spouse's help, women who work eight hours or more outside the home have two full-time jobs. But if their spouse works long hours or has a job requiring physical exertion or outside in the elements, it is not reasonable to expect that spouse to pitch in as much as they do. There must be a balance, and couples who love each other will make concessions to one another, depending upon their workload, hours, and working conditions.

Regardless of outside circumstances or influences, couples who recognize God as the head of their household will ask the Lord to help them meet their duties and to temper their attitudes. Compare the two versions of events, and the correct choice should be clear. It is up to each of us to develop the mindset we wish to present to others and to God. Even when we have stressful events and are rushing through life, we can choose what we say and do and how we act.

For the second scenario, let's consider how some additional "what if" facts about Janice, her family, and Cathy might affect the situation.

Todd has a demanding, stressful job, and recently, there has been more and more talk about the company being sold. He has no idea whether he will still have a job in six months – or six days. The company owner is coming in this morning for a mandated staff meeting. In Todd's experience, that kind of meeting is never a good sign.

The kids dread getting up. Mom has been yelling a lot lately, and they can't seem to do anything right. Dad is off in his own world, so Billy and Amanda feel scared and alone most of the time. Billy's grades have started to slip, and he's afraid to tell his parents that he made another D on a math test he took last week.

Amanda is becoming more withdrawn because the other girls have started bullying her at school. The only thing she knows to do is to try to stay in a protective shell. That strategy doesn't seem to be working at school or at home. As the children's mother, Janice could have impacted their lives by her own attitude and behavior. If she had reacted differently on a consistent basis, perhaps Billy's grades would be better, and maybe Amanda would have felt more secure at home and would not have withdrawn from the other girls at school. A withdrawn child becomes an easy target, and feeling more secure at home might have prevented the bullying altogether. At the very least, Amanda would have felt that she could tell her mother what was going on. If Todd had not been so preoccupied with his own worries, he might have noticed that something was amiss with his children. He would have had the opportunity to intervene and help the children before things got so far out of hand.

Cathy, a young woman with a husband who drinks too much, is stranded again. Her husband has stayed out at the bar all night, leaving her with no way to get to work and no idea when he is coming home. When she called Janice, she hated to ask for a favor again, but she was desperate, and her neighbor had already turned her down. Cathy was grateful that Janice had been understanding in the past and seemed to believe her reasons for not having a way to work. Cathy was too embarrassed to tell Janice the truth. Janice has no idea that Cathy is married to an alcoholic. Nobody knows how worried Cathy is about the financial fallout resulting from her husband's alcoholism and failure to stay sober and work on a consistent basis. Slamming the phone down in frustration, Cathy began to sob, reaching for her thin, worn coat for the six-block walk to the bus stop. She would be late again. She dreaded facing her supervisor. He had already warned her twice about coming to work late.

Hopefully most families aren't in totally negative situations like our make-believe family in the second example. But the truth is we never really know what someone else is going through or facing. If we did, we might be stunned at some people's situations. Knowing these additional facts sheds a bit more light on some of the reasons we don't always respond with love. But in both scenarios, the basic facts and circumstances were the same. So what made the difference? The difference was solely in the choices everyone made and the attitude they demonstrated. Each person could have chosen to set aside the apparent negativity of the moment, reach out to each other, and *decide* that they would focus on having faith that God would handle their burdens rather than getting caught up in the negativity. They could have refused to react in anger or fear. It is a choice, and the reactions and attitudes we choose will determine the flow of events. *As a man thinks, so is he.*

5. The Opposite of Love Is Not Hate

Many people might say that the opposite of love is hate. But is hatred really the opposite of love? Janice and her family love each other. She and Todd are usually loving toward one another, their children, co-workers, and others, and they are usually willing to help someone when they can. The problems that cropped up in the second scenario are not examples of hatred, but the emotions were definitely not loving or positive. So what is the opposite of love?

Some say it is indifference; others say the opposite of love is fear. I tend to agree with the latter. In the second scenario, Todd is afraid that he will lose his job. Janice fears that Todd is angry with her. Billy is afraid that his grades will get even worse, and Amanda is afraid of her classmates. Cathy fears that she won't be able to pay her family's bills and living expenses, plus she worries that she might lose her job because she's been late so many times.

That's a lot of fear! While fear does not take away the love, it obscures it and can cause doubt. In I John 4:18 (KJV), we learn that "There is no fear in love; but perfect love casteth out fear: because fear hath torment. He that feareth is not made perfect in love." Fear and love cannot co-exist. We must choose one or the other. Perfect love or tormenting fear? This would appear to be an easy choice, but many of us have allowed fear to torment our hearts and souls far too often. We can just as easily choose God's perfect love. Our spiritual health depends on the spiritual choices we make. We must choose wisely.

The Bible has much to say about fear. As Christians, should we be afraid? God says in Philippians 4:7 that we are to have peace that "transcends all understanding." Perhaps the bigger question is why we sometimes choose fear over simply believing God's Word. We willingly accept His love through the salvation that Jesus Christ offers, yet there are times when we choose fear over trusting God when it comes to everyday decisions and choices. We go to church and exclaim "Glory!" and "Hallelujah!" that God is able to do all things, yet we sometimes allow fear to override our faith. We are afraid that God can't do as his Word says, or we believe He can do all things, but we fear that He *won't* do it *for us*. We allow our fear to make the choice to doubt God. All the glory hallelujahs in the world won't replace the choices we make.

We study our Bibles and pray for God to show us His will. But how often do we read without comprehending, look without seeing, and speak God's Word to those around us without believing (Matthew 13:13)?

In spite of God's love for us and in spite of knowing that we are called to represent Christ and demonstrate His love to others, we sometimes choose to scurry back to the familiarity of fear. Any emotion that we choose over and over, whether it's positive or negative, becomes a habit. The habit will develop either way, but we have a choice over the habit we display in our lives, our thoughts, and our actions.

The good news is that, as long as we are breathing, it's never too late to turn from our sinful ways, and yes, it *is* a sin when we don't believe the promises and guidance in God's Word. How many of us walk around every day thinking that we are prayed up and studied up and living a Christian life when in reality we choose to dismiss God's Word about the peace He so lovingly offers? We sometimes choose desperation, fear, and doubt instead of God's blessed assurance that He is in control.

Even Jesus went through agony in the garden of Gethsemane, yet He still had peace that transcended all understanding (Matthew 26:36-45). He calmly stared death in the face, yet we can become totally stressed over minor daily circumstances. We *choose* not to believe that Jesus is offering peace, but He does much more than that. He *is* our peace!

6. The Many Faces of Love

The first step in loving our family, friends, and other people in our lives is to feel gratitude for them. By feeling grateful for others, we tend to have positive thoughts about them. We become more charitable toward them and more willing to overlook what we perceive as faults. In Rhonda Byrne's book, *The Magic,* she discusses what true gratitude is. Until I read her book, I considered myself a grateful person, but I now know that I was clueless when it came to gratitude. If you haven't read *The Magic,* I strongly encourage you to do so. (The book can be purchased from Amazon.com, or information is available on Byrne's website, www.thesecret.tv). The book is based on the Scripture found in the New Testament, "Whoever has will be given more; whoever does not have, even what they have will be taken from them," and features a series of exercises done over a 28-day period, designed to teach the meaning of true gratitude (Mark 4:25). The exercises show how to be thankful in all things, which is also one of God's commands to us (I Thessalonians 5:18). In one of the exercises, Byrne suggests thinking back to childhood and remembering all the various things that we didn't have to pay for – things that someone did for us, bought for us, or gave to us (p. 61-63).

Our parents provided food, shelter, clothing, and other things we needed. Teachers in school and at church went out of their way to help us learn. Our friends shared toys, books, and food with us. Our siblings stood by us and defended us. At work, mentors guided us and helped us to succeed. When we think of all the blessings that were given to us in love throughout our childhood and beyond, it is a

27

staggering realization. Love really is all around us, yet many times we don't even notice.

It would be impossible to list or even to recall every person who has blessed us along the way. In fact, it would be impossible even to *know* all the blessings we have received since birth. God showers blessings upon us each and every day, and He uses various situations and many different people to serve as His vessels. Just think how barren our lives would be without God's love!

Sometimes people bless us even when we are totally unaware of it. When I was in the sixth grade, one of the boys on our school bus was making "spit balls" – wadding up small bits of paper moistened with saliva and using a rubber band to "shoot" them at the girls on the bus. The very thought of spit balls was extremely gross to most girls. I somehow escaped being hit and I remember how happy I was that I was spared. It wasn't until years later that my brother, Jimmy, told me he had warned the other boy, "Do you see that little blonde headed girl up there?" When the boy nodded yes, my brother, who was older and bigger than the other boy, said, "Well, make sure you don't throw anything at her." The boy nodded, and I escaped the dreaded spit balls. That's a good example of someone blessing us without us even being aware of it. One of life's greatest blessings is having others pray for us, frequently without our knowledge. There's no way to know how often someone has petitioned Heaven's throne on our behalf and interceded for us. Only God knows. And how often, even when we were not displaying Godly love toward others as we should, has Jesus interceded for us (Romans 8:26, John 17)? That's an awesome realization!

Even though the world can be cold, callous, and cruel, there is still a lot of love shown every day. When we begin to think about all the many blessings we receive from others and feel truly grateful for them, we begin to see more blessings in our lives. Janice and her family had the opportunity to react with love or anger. All of us have that choice every day. Each choice, whether negative or positive, influences our lives and those around us. Our choices – *as a man thinks* – become our reality – *so is he.*

7. What Does Your Love Look Like?

Now is the time to think about our choices and understand what our love looks like to the other people in our lives, such as our family, friends, co-workers, and acquaintances. How does our love look to God?

There is a way to determine how our love appears to others, a test we can use to measure the amount of love we show. God's Word is frequently called our "guide book." It outlines the patterns we are to use in living our lives. Do we experience the pattern shown in I Corinthians 13? "Love is patient, love is kind...does not envy, does not keep a record of wrongs..." – if these examples of love do not show up in our lives, we can see that something is missing. We can see that our choices need to be reconsidered.

If we are Christ's ambassadors in this world, do others see Christ in us through our actions and speech? Do our co-workers see someone who is calm, kind, and generous, or do they hesitate to interact with us out of fear that we will "go off" on them in anger? Do our children see us as loving guides who want to help them be and do their best in life, or do they avoid talking to us out of fear that we will be judgmental and angry? Or even worse, do our children automatically know, based on previous experience, that we will be "too busy" to have time for them? Do our spouses see us as a balm to soothe away the day's stresses and an oasis where they can be refreshed when times are difficult, or do they suffer in silence because they feel they can't relax around us or tell us how they really feel or what they really think?

The situations I'm talking about are not extraordinary. I'm talking about everyday life. On an average day, do we try to reach out to others and show God's love?

Here's the acid test:

Before we think, whatever we are in the habit of thinking, would we think those thoughts if we knew that Jesus was aware of them? (He is, by the way.)

Before we speak, whatever we plan to say, would we make those statements to Jesus?

Before we act or react, whatever our normal actions and reactions are, would we react that way to Jesus? Whatever we do to the least of those in His kingdom, we do to Him (Matthew 25:40).

In spite of not always being easy, it really is that simple. And it really is a choice. A simple choice. What will each of us choose today?

8. Showing Love to Family and Friends

Tomorrow, from the second we wake up until the second we go to sleep, we all have a multitude of simple choices to make. I'm not suggesting that it's always easy to choose what God would have us to choose. Life, other people, and our own shortcomings get in the way. But here are some questions that will surely give us something to think about.

If someone says or does something that hurts us or makes us angry, instead of reacting, are we willing to take a few seconds to count to ten before responding or to silently whisper a prayer for this person? Consider how long Jesus must wait for us, even when we do something to hurt Him, but the Bible teaches in John 17 that He prays for us anyway.

When a family member does something annoying like leaving the cap off the toothpaste or not taking a dirty glass to the kitchen, are we willing to overlook it, to replace the cap or take the glass to the sink ourselves? Can we forget for just that one moment that we've asked them a hundred times to put the toothpaste cap back on or take dirty glasses to the kitchen? Can we be more concerned with kindness than we are with what's fair? Doesn't Jesus do that for us when we fail to do something we know we should? If we "study" His Word yet choose to disregard or disobey its guidance – His *commands* – isn't that the same as when someone we love chooses to ignore our will?

If a co-worker takes credit for an idea we had, are we willing to pray for them privately while speaking well of them publicly? Every good and perfect gift comes from God (James 1:17). How many things do we expect, or even demand, while thinking that we get them on our own? Jesus blesses us, not only with His provision to us, but He also speaks well of us when He prays to the Father, in spite of what we have claimed we did on our own. If every good and perfect gift comes from the Lord, it is His blessing at work, not anything we have done.

If one of our children exhibits behavior problems, are we willing to sit and talk to them, hold them close, tell them we love them, and ask how we can help? Doesn't Jesus do this for us every time we forget that Christians are to walk in love and forgive our enemies? How many times do we allow our stubborn pride to keep us from acting like a believer? In spite of our unbelief and un-Christ-like behavior, Jesus holds us close and forgives us when we ask.

If a friend is taking advantage of our good nature yet again, are we willing to turn the other cheek? In Matthew 18:22 (KJV), the Bible says we are to turn the other cheek seven times seventy – *are we willing to do it even once?* How often do we take Jesus for granted? How often every day does He have to turn the other cheek to us?

If a spouse is taxing our nerves by complaining about a friend or co-worker for the umpteenth time, and we know they have no intention of addressing the issues directly, are we willing to listen anyway? Imagine how Jesus must feel when we keep bringing the same old problems up to Him over and over. Didn't He say we can cast our burdens at His feet and let Him handle them (Psalm 55:22, I Peter 5:7)? Why do we hang onto them and keep asking Him to take care of them when we won't turn them loose? Jesus patiently listens even when He has heard the same complaint or request repeatedly, in spite of our claim that we have left our burdens with Him.

And here's the really big question: Are we willing to take a long, hard look at the way we react and respond to Jesus? He said if we love Him, we will keep His commandments (John 14:15). If we choose not to keep

His commandments, it's the same as telling Him, "I know what You said I should do, but I am going to ignore You and do what I want." Why do we want our own way, and why are we unwilling to even consider what someone else might need? If our speech, actions, and behavior aren't perfect, why do we expect perfection from others?

All the examples above are situations and attitudes that frequently occur to most of us. Every time we become upset, angry, frustrated, irritated, fed up, or any of the other myriad of negative emotions out there, we have a chance to *choose*. Only we, with God's help, have the power to make that choice.

When it comes to choices, there are only two. We will always choose one or the other, even if it's by default. When we don't make a clear choice to do what Jesus would do, by default we are choosing the opposite.

The Bible says we should choose life (Deuteronomy 30:19). If we can respond the way Jesus would, isn't that the best way to choose life, a life that is fulfilled and joyful, a life that demonstrates *agape* to others and to the Lord? Are we willing to choose life today?

9. God's Definition

Agape – the ultimate love – is God's definition of love. God's love is sacrificial. When Jesus hung on the cross, His love was selfless – He was the sacrificial Lamb. He tenderly demonstrates that kind of love to us on a daily basis. Sometimes I wonder if God grows weary waiting on His children to grasp the depth of His love, but one of His greatest gifts and blessings to all mankind is that He doesn't grow weary. He is Love, personified – patient, kind, does not envy, does not boast, is not proud, honors others, is not self-seeking, is not easily angered, and keeps no record of wrongs (I Corinthians 13:4-7). He wants us – *commands* us – to personify love, too.

God did not only tell us He loves us. His love alone would be enough, but God went to great lengths to show us His love. We were born to love and worship Him, so one could say that God loved each of us into existence. But that was only the beginning. He loved us so much that He sent His only Son to die an excruciating death on Calvary's cross to atone for our sins (John 3:16). Jesus took our place on the cross, the ultimate act of sacrificial love.

Neither God nor Jesus had to do what they did for us. They did it without hesitation simply because they loved us with a real love. If God's tremendous sacrifice for us was not enough, Jesus agreed to give His life on the cross, willingly dying for our sins in a final act of love that was only the beginning of eternal life for every believer. But God the Father and God the Son were just getting started. God took His Son to Glory, but He did not leave us to fend for ourselves. In His great love and mercy, He left God the Holy Spirit here to be with us always, to dwell within us, and to comfort us (John 14:16-17). That, my friend, is real love – *agape*.

If that is God's definition of love, shouldn't it be ours as well? Shouldn't we be patient, kind, and loving, even when others are not thinking, speaking, or behaving as we think they should? Who are we to make those judgments about someone else's actions? To paraphrase Plato, "Be kinder than necessary because everyone you meet is fighting some kind of battle." We don't know what someone goes through every day. The Bible teaches, "So in everything, do to others what you would have them do to you..." (Matthew 7:12). If we go through a difficult time personally, we want patience, sympathy, and understanding from others, but are we equally willing to give that same patience, sympathy, and understanding in return? Only when we are able to do that can we say that we know what real love is.

10. Love Is a Red and White Umbrella

I want to share an incident that happened when my husband, Wayne, and I were newlyweds. It is the perfect example of finding love in everyday places. While the circumstances were not extraordinary, the incident clearly demonstrates the meaning of true love. Before I share it, I want to provide some background information.

Wayne has always been so kind, sweet, and patient. I was a mess emotionally when we met, and God has used Wayne's steady, patient love to help heal many of the emotional wounds I experienced long before we met.

My family lived in poverty, and most of the time, we all just tried to survive. Poverty tends to place people in the role of being a victim. Without money, many of life's choices are unavailable to us. We begin to assume that we have no choices about anything. Life just happens, and all we can do is try to make the best of it. If I could change anything about my family and my childhood, it would be for my parents to provide spiritual guidance and instruction early on through God's Word and to teach us that we always have choices. *Always.*

Let me take a moment to make clear that I do not blame or judge my parents. I know that they loved my siblings and me, without a doubt. In fact, some of my siblings have very different memories of our childhoods. It's possible, even likely, that they might not agree with my assessment, but our perception determines our reality. I can speak only for myself, and based on my memories and experiences during childhood, my reality was feeling unloved. Yet I'm aware that my parents provided for me, wanted me to do well in school, and tried to teach me life lessons, such as honesty, kindness, generosity, and other positive traits. Still, much was missing on an emotional and spiritual level, at least from my perspective. I know they did all that they knew to do. If someone doesn't know how to do something, they can't demonstrate or teach it to others. Like everyone else, they were a product of their upbringing, shaped largely by their family environment as children. But I've wondered over the years how different all of our lives might have been if we had been nurtured more often and had heard "I love you," or "you're a great kid," or similar words of encouragement. How different would my parents' lives have been if they had experienced more nurturing and encouragement as children?

As a child, I didn't realize many of the problems in my family. But as an adult, I can look back and see the pain, hardships, poverty, and emotional and spiritual ignorance that sometimes permeated our lives.

Growing up without ever receiving hugs or hearing, "I love you," not even once that I can recall, some of my siblings and I were not always able to form healthy ideas about love and how to show it. The frequent lack of affection and nurturing created many problems for all of us. Like some of my siblings, I had relationship problems through the years. As a child, I felt invisible to those around me. As an adult, I understand that I was not invisible, and that I did matter to my family, regardless of the way I perceived childhood. But how we *feel* trumps what we *know*, and it is hard to erase a feeling that has been ingrained into my psyche for as long as I can remember. Playing an old phonograph record over and over creates a groove in the vinyl that causes the record to spin in the same spot over and over. In the same way, emotions can end up endlessly replaying in our minds. This is true whether the emotions are positive or negative. I'm thankful that the

Lord and my husband have done so much to heal a hurtful past.

When Wayne and I met, I had never known anyone like him. He always had a smile and a joke to tell. After meeting him, I felt like I had been led into the sunlight. When anyone has been in the dark literally, spiritually, or emotionally, the intensity of coming into the light can seem overwhelming.

Prior to meeting Wayne, I had become convinced that God must have wanted me to live my life alone. I decided that even though I didn't want to go through life alone, perhaps I needed to accept this way of life as God's will for me. I resisted Wayne's initial attempts to get to know me, but he slowly kept reaching out to me until I finally took his hand. That was one of the smartest things I've ever done. I feel incredibly blessed to have him in my life. Not only is he a wonderful father to his own two children, he has done so much for my daughters during the years he and I have been married.

What I want to share is commonplace, and some might think it is inconsequential. Yet it is a perfect example of using routine situations to find God's love in everyday places.

Wayne and I had been married just a couple of months. He got home from work every day about an hour before I did, and he usually had supper cooked by the time I got home. This alone was astounding to me because it was definitely a new experience.

One evening on the way home, a fierce thunderstorm occurred, pouring rain down so fast until it was difficult to see the road. I finally made it to the parking lot of our apartment building. I did not have an umbrella in the car, so I planned to wait until the rain slacked up and then make a break for the breezeway of the apartment building.

I sat quietly, waiting for the rain to slow down. Through the blurring rain, I became aware of a flash of red. At first I could not tell what it was. Gradually, I realized that it was my precious husband, standing under the breezeway, waiting for me to notice that he was there. Waiting for me to see that he had a huge red and white umbrella. *Waiting ... for me.*

When he saw that I noticed him, he dashed to the car and opened the door, held the umbrella over my head, and held me closely as we both ran back under the breezeway. That was such a sweet gesture, and to me it is a perfect example of *agape* – sacrificial love. Wayne didn't care if he got wet. He didn't care if he had to wait on me to see him. The only thing he cared about was helping me avoid getting soaked and to get safely inside our home to spend time with him. He sacrificed his own comfort and convenience to help me. He *loved* me.

It's true that there are seven billion people on Planet Earth, and they might have at least seven billion definitions of love. That's all well and good. But as for my own definition, now you know why I am certain that love is a red and white umbrella.

Epilogue

To all the parents out there, I want to speak directly to you. The purpose of this book is to point out what can happen when parents are unable, for whatever reason, to address their children's emotional and spiritual needs or to teach them the meaning of God's love. The best way to show God's love is to ensure your children's spiritual education and growth. Seek out a church that teaches the Bible's truths, and take your children to church. Be spiritual leaders and set the example of the importance of hearing God's Word preached and of meeting with other believers for fellowship and encouragement. Get your children involved – the younger, the better – in church activities. Many churches have children's programs that teach God's Word in ways that children can understand, no matter how young they are. Children can also learn how to use their gifts and talents, such as singing, playing an instrument, helping the teacher, etc. This builds their self-esteem while teaching them that all gifts and talents should be used to glorify the Lord.

While churches are important, it is ultimately up to you, dear parents, to ensure your children's spiritual growth and emotional health. Teach your children about Jesus and what He did for all of us and what it means for them personally. Take the time and make the effort to ensure your children's emotional stability and positive self-esteem. Make sure they mature in faith and increase their trust in and dependence upon God. Otherwise, they will be doomed to live in emotional and spiritual poverty, and they will be unequipped to understand or recognize real love or to show it properly. This kind of poverty can have lifelong

41

consequences that are sometimes catastrophic. My hope is that I can warn parents and help prevent an emotional and spiritual deficit in their own families. Take the time to know your children, talk to them, *see* them, and let them know that they matter. Teach them that they are a unique and special gift from God. Then give them the gift of *your* time. It will be a priceless treasure in their lives.

The sooner children become emotionally and spiritually mature, the better able they are to make choices that lead to a happy, productive life. As an adult, I understand that my family loves me, but as a child I felt like I was in the way, just another burden to parents who, along with their resources, were already stretched too thin. With my siblings, the age difference (from five to fifteen years) was a huge factor. They were busy living life, and what seemed like indifference to me then was only their efforts to survive and have a life of their own. In my childish mind, however, becoming invisible was my way of coping, to take myself out of the way. Because I felt invisible, I tended to shy away from social situations and to feel uncomfortable around others. To a child's reasoning, feeling invisible = unimportance. I didn't matter. Even though my family loved me, because I didn't *feel* loved on an emotional level, *being unloved* became my reality. Our perception of reality, whether it is correct or not, becomes the driving force in our lives.

Feeling unloved or unimportant leads to timidity and creates so many problems that follow a child far into adulthood. Don't assume that a child feels loved. Make sure they know that they matter and are loved deeply, unconditionally, by telling them and showing them. In addition to providing spiritual instruction, help your children to develop healthy self-esteem. Children absorb very quickly what they are taught or what they live at home. By emphasizing your children's value to you and to God and teaching God's truths to them, you can ensure that what they absorb will serve them well for a lifetime.

So, parents, show *agape* love to your children. Respect them and teach them to respect themselves. Teach them that life doesn't have to just happen to them. Help them to see that they have choices, and then discuss the choices with them. Explain the choices that God would have them make, and encourage them to choose God's way. Just spending time with a child helps them to feel loved. In turn, this nurtures their self-esteem. Spending time while teaching and promoting God's Word helps not only their self-esteem, but it also colors their view of love in a Godly way, and it helps them to make wise choices all their lives.

I want to convey the concept that in order to recognize God's love in everyday places, we have to experience it in everyday places. Even an adult who was taught nothing of God's love as a child can learn about it now and show it to others, especially to their own children, on a daily basis. If I can prevent one soul from going through the emotional trauma my family has experienced, as well as all the negativity that followed, then my purpose here will be accomplished. While it isn't easy to share deep, inner thoughts, my desire to help others is stronger than my reluctance to share personal feelings and perceptions. I'm convinced that the devastating events I experienced 20 years ago could have been avoided with a more mature emotional and spiritual mindset. It's one of the reasons I want to share my story, to help someone else avoid such experiences.

At the same time, I don't want to dishonor my parents or my family. We all did the best we could with the resources and knowledge we had. My mother was one of the smartest people I've ever known, period. She endured tremendous hardships and heartache. Her first child was stillborn, but not due to any illness or condition of the baby. My mother, a tiny woman, was having a difficult birth. The baby was too large to descend through the birth canal. This was at a time when people had their babies at home. Even though my parents repeatedly called and pleaded with the doctor to come and help my mother, he never showed up. They had no money and no insurance, so money and the doctor's time were apparently more important and worth more than a mother's difficulty or a child's life. A perfectly healthy, beautiful baby girl smothered in the birth canal waiting to be born, killed by poverty and a doctor's indifference.

I'm sure this event took a huge emotional toll on my parents, especially my mother. The loss of a child to a mother who has carried the child for nine months is a tragedy that forever touches her heart and soul. Perhaps this deep hurt caused her to stifle her emotions and numbly get through many years of struggling in poverty. Until the day my mother died, she carried in her wallet a worn and yellowed newspaper clipping about the death of her firstborn. She went on to have seven children who lived, but she still had very little money. This makes the amazing job she did all the more noteworthy because she did it with only her ingenuity and resourcefulness. My father was also extremely smart and industrious. He always worked hard and provided for us the best he could. They taught us well with the things they understood, but they simply were unaware of the importance of ensuring spiritual and emotional health. If a child's life is devoid of such guidance, the line from Dorothy Law Nolte's poem, "A child learns what they live," can be achingly true.

The intent of the book is to teach parents, and all those who will become parents, that what happens in a child's life can have far reaching and potentially destructive consequences when emotional and spiritual needs are ignored. It bears repeating that just meeting a child's basic needs for food, clothing, and shelter is not enough. In order to have a healthy attitude toward love, a child's emotional needs are just as important as any other, and meeting their spiritual needs is even more important because they have eternal consequences. I also want people to realize that they can change the effects of their childhood, to overcome their roots and their upbringing by understanding God's love.

We receive God's love by repenting of our sins, asking for forgiveness, and accepting His Son, Jesus Christ, into our hearts. I want people to understand that Christians are bound by His commandments to show love – *agape* – to others in order to bless the world with His love and draw people to Him. May the Lord ever be high and lifted up in our lives, and may we show true love to family, friends, acquaintances – and the world.

About the Author

Diane Simmons Dill is a Bessemer, Alabama native who loves writing and encouraging others. Retired from the U. S. Treasury Department and the U. S. Coast Guard Reserve, Diane now has time to write, and she loves to inspire others through her work. She specializes in non-fiction, but she is equally at home writing fiction and poetry. She also enjoys writing songs and singing and making jewelry and soy wax candles.

Diane offers services for editing, copywriting, ghostwriting, and other writing projects through her company, RightWrite Productions ("Get it *Right* When You Write!") For more information, or to book her for a speaking engagement, please contact her via email or Facebook, listed below.

Diane graduated cum laude and with University Honors from the University of Alabama at Birmingham in 2010, with a B. A. in English (Creative Writing) and a minor in Art (Graphic Design). Diane lives near Birmingham, Alabama with her extremely sweet and wonderful husband, Wayne, and their two ridiculously spoiled cats, Maddie and Abby.

Email: ddill50@gmail.com
www.facebook.com/rightwriteproductions

A Request

Thank you for reading my book! My prayer is that you were blessed and uplifted by it.

If you enjoyed the book and would be kind enough to write a review, I would deeply appreciate it. Thank you, and blessings to you!

References:

Byrne, Rhonda. The Magic. New York: Atria Books, 2012. Print.

Website: www.thesecret.tv

Quotes taken from www.goodreads.com.